CW00376305

ISBN 978-1-3999-4854-8

First published in Great Britain in 2023
Skillshub Ltd
5 Orchard Court
Binley Business Park
Coventry
CV3 2TQ

Contents

Introduction

As learning and development (L&D) professionals we are all under pressure to do "more with less" and pull the occasional rabbit out of the hat when it comes to the learning solutions that we provide for our people.

We are positioned as the department that can transform our people and really add value to our organisation. But at the same time, we are the first ones to be cut when there's a recession, a downturn in demand, or dare I say the pandemic word!

It's weird, isn't it?

I fundamentally believe that the way we position our learning and development functions is wrong. We do not just "offer training". We are much more than that! We are about performance improvement, and it's a mission critical function, not a nice to have.

But where is the proof?

Where is the hard evidence that we're adding real, tangible results to our organisations? Most cannot provide anything other than happy sheet output and the occasional uplift in employee survey results.

For me, learning and development is all about creating an impact. It's about creating an impact in results!

And that's what this book is about. We are going to look at why this is so important at an organisational and learning event.

I'm also going to specifically look at how learning management systems are currently being perceived, and why more emphasis should be placed on learning transfer than the number of logins that are made.

I'll then cover some learning evaluation models and some alternatives to Kirkpatrick!

Here, I'll highlight different models that can help you measure the effectiveness of your learning and development strategy against your organisational goals and objectives.

I'll then wrap up with 50 questions that you can ask yourself, to help you move away from learning consumption and move to a performance orientated learning and development powerhouse.

Ready to make an impact? Let's go!

Sean McPheat – CEO

Contact

Web: www.skillshub.com
Email: info@skillshub.com
Phone: 02476 998 101

Chapter 1

Is Usage of any Use at all?

"The way we position an LMS needs to change".

Sean McPheat

The whole idea for this book came about from a conversation that I had with a Learning and Development Manager of a major corporation. We were chatting about the learning management system that they had for their people.

The conversation went something like this:

L&D Manager
"Our people aren't taking enough courses on our LMS. They need to be taking more courses and resources."

Me
"What makes you say that?"

L&D Manager
"Well, on average only 21% of our people have logged in during the last quarter."

Me
"And what results are you seeing?"

L&D Manager
"Oh, the average assessment mark at the end of each session is 98%. We have 100% completion rates too."

Me
"Sorry, I meant results back in the workplace. The impact."

L&D Manager
"Oh, well they enjoy the learning they take. I assume it's making a difference, but I wish they would take some more courses and be more engaged. Our current LMS is not proving a good return on investment."

Me
"You mention that your LMS is not proving a good return on investment, could I just ask you a quick question around that?

Would you rather have someone take 1 course per week and be very highly engaged with your LMS but make no improvements to themselves or the business, or someone who took 1 course per quarter and saved the company £50,000, reduced staff attrition in their team by 2 FTE, and improved morale by 20% on their team staff satisfaction score?"

That scenario is more common than you think.

Too many of us get hung up about usage and do not spend enough time on the transfer or implementation of the learning within the workplace. The purpose of digital learning or an LMS is to not just to consume the course or resource. The purpose is to do something with what you have learnt.

Therefore, **the objective of learning is performance improvement**. It's not learning for learning's sake.

Too many organisations are fixated on purchasing learning solutions without really understanding where the skills gaps are and what performance areas need improving.

LMS's are the flavour of the month, so by default some organisations think they need one without any data or needs analysis being completed up front.

What happens then?

An LMS gets deployed without any proper strategy or links to performance improvement, it doesn't get used, and it's then classed as a failure.

An expensive failure!

When I ask organisations what their KPI's are for their learning management system (if, indeed they have any at all), they normally come out with the following:

- Usage - The number of courses, content and resources that are being consumed and by who.

- Completion - How many learners complete the course/resource.

- Assessment - For those learners that do complete the course/ resource, what are their assessment scores.

- Evaluation - Do the learners think the courses and resources are useful and engaging.

- Time - How many times did the learners log into the platform and how long did they spend on there.

That's okay but...

Surely, one of the most important KPI's should be around the impact that the learning has made - whatever your definition of impact is. Those KPI's above are simple to measure. That's why they are measured!

Let's take a closer look at this!

Lisa Turner works in your organisation, and she is one of the 250 learners that has access to your LMS. Below are her usage statistics over the last 12 months.

Take a moment to look over everything:

She logged into the LMS a total of 4 times over the 12 months. All those logins were made within 2 months out of the 12. She opened 3 resources, took 4 courses, and spent a total time of just 90 minutes within the LMS which equates to an average of 7 ½ minutes per month.

Now, do you think the LMS has done its job for Lisa?

Learners like this are constantly pigeonholed as not being engaged with the system but is this true?

The LMS could in fact be playing more of a role than first meets the eye.

We asked Lisa what action she had taken after one of the courses and below is a summary.

Course 1 – Running an effective one-to-one meeting.

Before this course, Lisa's team were having two, one-to-one meetings with her each year.

The sessions were more like a general chat with no focus or structure.

After the course Lisa:

- Created a one-to-one template one for her team and one for herself to complete to prepare for each one-to-one.

- Created a template for recording the output and actions from each session.

- **Scheduled monthly one-to-ones** for each of her team.

- **Conducted her one-to-ones** with more structure and purpose based on the learning from the course – this enabled her to have better quality conversations based on objectives.

Lisa did a lot of work after the course.

Whilst the learning itself lasted approximately 20 minutes for that one course, the implementation and actions from the learning took much longer.

To take this a step further we asked Lisa and her team what the impact was from the changes that she had made to this.

Here are just some of the outputs:

- During the year Lisa held **90, structured one-to-one sessions** with her team across 10 people. The previous year she only held 21 in total.

- Her team felt more motivated and focused because of the changes in the structure and approach. They felt that **the effectiveness of the approach was now 88% compared to 34% before the changes**.

- Lisa demonstrated that **85% of all objectives were met** from the team whereas last year only 35% of objectives were met.

- One of Lisa's team was thinking of leaving 12 months ago because of the lack of clarity in their role and specific goals. Now, they are more motivated than ever (**saving £4,500 in recruitment fees**, the time taken to recruit, and the added workload placed on others until someone is found).

- One of Lisa's team managed to **renegotiate a contract and save the organisation £25,000** based on the structured work they completed during their one-to-one meetings – this would never have happened before as the development and coaching was spread over several sessions.

From that one piece of learning, Lisa made a big impact on her team and the organisation.

Based on usage her engagement was ranked as **slow**, but in terms of the impact she has made on the business - she is a **legend!**

The LMS did its role!

Lisa identified a need to improve her performance, and she took a relevant course/resource. She then did something with the learning. That is the most important thing.

We've all got to remember that an LMS is a resource. It's a resource to help us and should not be judged solely on its usage statistics.

Sure, we need to gather those figures to look at the quality of the resources but **ultimately it should be down to the impact that those resources have had on the learner and the organisation.**

Performance and impact metrics are important because they provide evidence of the impact of the learning on your organisation. They can demonstrate the return on investment (ROI) of your LMS and digital solutions, by showing how the training has led to cost savings, increased productivity, increased sales, or any other measurable improvements in the organisation.

For example, if an organisation implements a sales training programme through an LMS, performance statistics such as increased sales revenue or a higher close rate can demonstrate the effectiveness of the training and its impact on the organisation.

Similarly, if a company provides safety training through an LMS, performance statistics such as a reduction in accidents or injuries can demonstrate the effectiveness of the programme.

There are a variety of KPI's that can be measured to demonstrate the impact that an LMS has on an organisation, so here are a few examples:

- Increased Sales.
- Increased Productivity.
- Reduced Costs.
- Increased Employee Retention.

- Reduction In accidents.
- Improved Customer Satisfaction.
- Increased Efficiency.
- Improved Quality.
- Increased Compliance.
- Increased Job Satisfaction.
- Increased Proficiency.
- Improved Time Management.
- Improved Teamwork.
- Increased Innovation.
- Increased Adaptability.
- Increased Creativity.
- Improved Decision Making.
- Improved Problem Solving.
- Improved Work Quality.
- Reduced Error Rate.
- Increased Sales Conversion.
- Reduced Employee Turnover.
- Increased Employee Engagement.
- Improved Inventory Management.
- Increased Operational Efficiency.
- Improved Leadership Skills.
- Increased Professional Development.
- Improved Communication Skill.
- Increased Technological Proficiency.

Chapter 2

Shifting the Focus of your LMS

"It's got to move away from Usage and on to Impact".

Sean McPheat

"What's the purpose of your LMS?"

It's a question I have asked hundreds of L&D Managers over the years.

I can tell you that a high majority of them respond with the following:

- "To provide learning at scale".
- "To provide a cost-effective learning solution".
- "To provide learning to our people who are all over the world".
- "To create a new initiative to promote staff development".

Hardly any of them respond with "To improve performance".

There's an initial focus on the delivery of learning and how that is completed, and then the quality of the content and the platform follows.

Questions LMS providers get asked include:

- How many courses do you offer?
- What format are they in?
- What reporting does your LMS have?
- Is your LMS user friendly?

Questions are predominately focused on features.

Now of course they are important, but better questions to ask would be:

- How are your courses structured so they will improve the performance of our people?
- What tools and resources does your content or LMS offer to help transfer the learning into the workplace?
- How does your LMS measure what content is having the biggest impact within our business?
- How does your LMS create a learning journey that is measurable?

You see how these questions are geared more around performance rather than features? By asking these types of questions you will get to see how the LMS can contribute to having an impact within the workplace, whilst understanding the features better.

EXERCISE

Think about the **performance related questions** that you could ask your existing or prospective LMS provider.

Ask them how each feature has been designed and created to improve performance rather than just the feature itself. It's a mindset thing. But a very important one.

A Shift in Emphasis and Focus

From Usage to Impact

Once you understand each of the features from a performance improvement perspective it's a lot easier to sell the benefits of your LMS and its content.

Your learners want to know "what's in it for them?"

EXERCISE

List all the features of the content you use and the functionality of your LMS.

Write down **how each one helps to transfer the learning** or ultimately improve the performance of the learner (there will be some that are not applicable).

If you can **set impact objectives** for your learners **rather than usage objectives**, then they will approach what they learn in a completely different way. Usage measures how often the system is being used, which does not necessarily indicate its effectiveness.

Additionally, a system that is designed to improve performance will likely also have high usage, as users will find it valuable and useful.

A system that prioritises performance over usage is **more likely to be aligned with the overall goals and objectives** of your organisation.

On the other hand, a system that prioritises usage may include features that are more focused on user engagement and adoption, such as social networking tools, but may not directly contribute to the improvement of learner outcomes.

Usage should never be used as the sole metric for evaluating a LMS because it does not provide a complete picture of the system's effectiveness. Usage measures how often the system is being used, which does not necessarily indicate its impact on your learners and engagement. A system with high usage may not be providing the intended benefits, while a system with low usage may still be effective in improving learner outcomes.

Additionally, usage does not consider factors such as user engagement and satisfaction, which are also important indicators of a system's effectiveness.

High usage does not guarantee that users are engaged or satisfied with the system. A system may have high usage, but users may not be using it in the intended way or may not be enjoying the experience.

Furthermore, a system's usage can be artificially inflated by factors such as mandatory use or lack of alternative options. If a system is being used solely because it's required by the institution, it does not necessarily indicate that it's useful or effective.

Evidence-Based Data

A system that prioritises performance is more likely to be data-driven and evidence-based, which can help ensure that the system is continually updated and improved based on feedback and evaluation.

This can lead to a more effective and efficient use of resources, as well as better outcomes for learners.

Show evidence of the system's effectiveness: Share data and evidence of the system's effectiveness with stakeholders. This can help to build trust and confidence in the system and demonstrate the value of prioritising performance over usage.

The Course Thumbnail of the Future

Here's my vision for the future and what we're working towards at Skillshub. Forget about likes and shares for a moment and think about a course thumbnail (below) that has the average impacts and results that your learners have recorded by taking that course.

The above means:

♥ **97%**	Quality of the course
⏱ **33%**	Average time savings and productivity improvement
£ **245k↑**	Increase in sales + reduction in costs
🎯 **88%**	An overall impact rating based on all criteria

Naturally, engagement levels will improve if your learners know that their productivity could be increased by an average of 33% by taking this course. This is far more meaningful than a course having 24 likes and 2 shares.

Chapter 3

Moving from Logins to Learning Transfer

"Logging on 50 times is pointless unless you are going to do something with the learning".

Sean McPheat

Have you ever discussed the meaning of life with your family and friends?

No, me neither! But I bet the discussion could have gone on for hours.

In terms of L&D, have you ever discussed with your learners, your colleagues, and stakeholders what the purpose of learning is?

That conversation, in theory, should be quite short.

Apart from those self-development junkies who like to learn for the sake of it, mostly for enjoyment and do nothing with their newfound knowledge.

The purpose of learning, in my opinion should be a no-brainer.

The purpose of learning is performance improvement - *that's it in a nutshell!*

Once you and everyone else around you understand that and buys into that, the whole way you look at learning solutions changes.

The judge, jury, and executioner as to how useful learning has been, comes down to its impact on the person and on the organisation.

It's not about consumption.

It's not about the quantity of learning.

Instead, it's about the quality of the learning, how timely it is and ultimately, the impact it has.

Let me ask you a few questions so you can gauge where your emphasis is right now:

- Do you focus a lot of importance on usage statistics with your LMS?
- Are you wracking your brains on how to get your learners engaged with your LMS?

- Do you produce a lot of reports on the types and numbers of courses your learners take?

- Do you place importance on quiz and assessment results?

- How much time do you spend on helping your learners to transfer their knowledge into the workplace?

- What resources do you offer them to help with this?

- Do you measure the impact and ROI of your training solutions?

- How do you measure its effectiveness? Which method do you use?

- Do your key stakeholders and budget holders understand the impact that your learning and development solutions are making on the organisation?

- Do you know which courses, resources and solutions have the biggest return on investment for your organisation?

Answering those questions gives you a quick indication as to whether you're focusing more on consumption or end results.

Give yourself an overall score out of 100 of how much focus, energy and importance is placed on the end results of your learning solutions. (100 being most)

_____ out of 100

Transferring Learning into Performance

Earlier, I mentioned that the objective of learning is not learning, it's performance improvement and that we shouldn't be learning for the sake of it.

Instead, learning should have an end product to reach that is much more than just increased knowledge.

The learning that you provide for your people, both formal and informal, should be closely linked to business outcomes and objectives.

We see so many L&D departments put on a suite of courses or offer the latest and greatest LMS packed full of content, but eventually they all get lead down the same rabbit hole and contribute to no significant changes in performance.

It all becomes a waste of money.

What happens then?

Your workplace may assume that "L&D doesn't work."

You then run the risk of your training budget being cut. Without having performance improvements to back up your training, L&D will be seen as a cost rather than an investment.

What can be done to bridge the gap between learning and improving performance?

The answer is the transfer of learning! So, let's look at what this is and discuss ways to achieve this.

What is meant by the Transfer of Learning?

Learning transfer is what your learners do with their newfound knowledge or skills to improve their performance.

It's all about how to encourage, promote and evaluate the transfer of knowledge, skills, and behaviours from training into the workplace.

We've all been guilty of reading a self-development book and then doing absolutely nothing with all this new "wisdom" and learning we now have. We're not transferring this learning into our work to improve the performance of what we're doing.

We've all been on that course (this is an example of formal learning) that required us to take multiple days out of our work schedule but then done nothing off the back of it.

We've all been guilty of seeing a colleague perform well at work (this is an example of informal learning) and saying to ourselves that we're going to use a similar strategy in the future, but again it's forgotten by lunchtime.

Then there's the LMS surfer who bounces around your platform like they are on Netflix, dipping in here, watching a bit there, and doing nothing at all afterwards.

This frequent occurrence is a major concern for learning and development departments around the world.

The transfer of learning sparks varying debates on how much learning should be applied in the workplace for it to be classed as effective and how learning transfer should be measured.

For example, how much learning transfer is enough and is it the quantity or the outcome that is most important?

For example, Skillshub's parent company, the MTD Training Group, ran a leadership programme for a company where **one manager negotiated a contract of materials down by £250,000** and could pinpoint the exact technique, they implemented from the negotiation resources they learned from the programme.

Despite this, they freely admitted that they did not implement as much of the learning as they should have.

Conversely, there were scores of managers who made small, incremental changes that impacted morale, confidence, time savings, revenue generation, reductions in health and safety incidents, and lower staff attrition.

This goes to show that although big headlines like the £250,000 are one way to show learning transfer, small yet incremental business outcomes are also important for it to be measured.

We hear all the time of L&D managers quoting arbitrary figures that 60% or 80% of the learning needs to be embedded into the workplace.

However, if this isn't enforced and employees aren't given the time, resources, and support to enable them to use their learning in the workplace, it would be unjust and unhelpful to expect those kinds of results.

Not only that, but some people are so overworked with tasks, emails, and responsibilities that they never have the time or energy to implement what they have learned.

For professional learning and development managers, measuring the transfer of learning should all be about business outcomes.

Let's look at the benefits of Learning Transfer.

What are the benefits of Learning Transfer?

If learning is transferred into the workplace and used, then there should be lots of benefits to be had.

When figuring out what learning and development activities you offer, you should really start with the benefits in mind and the business outcomes you want to achieve and work backwards from there, rather than the other way around.

- Improved productivity
- Higher staff engagement rates.
- Reduced staff attrition.
- Improved customer service.
- Higher revenues and profits.
- Reduced costs.
- Increased morale.
- Better motivation.
- Increased confidence levels.

All the above are generic improvements and if you're creating proper training needs then there will be a lot of niche business outcomes that are unique to your organisation too.

For example, we worked with a railway company and a couple of their unique business outcomes included:

- Reduced number of **accidents** on their platforms.
- Reduced number of **fatalities**.
- Reduced number of **H&S incidents** at their stations.
- **Gold standard** for Investors in People accreditation.

Your business outcomes will include generic benefits as well as niche benefits and your training solutions will need to reflect these objectives and ultimately provide the knowledge, skills and behaviours that will contribute to achieving the outcomes you desire.

How can you measure the Transfer of Learning?

In terms of your L&D department:

- Which of your learning events and resources have the biggest impact on your business?
- Do you know what type of training gives you the best results?
- Is it face to face, elearning, coaching or online resources?
- Now think about your LMS; which course or resource has the biggest impact on your business?

Can you answer those questions with real, tangible evidence?

These are the type of questions that you need hard and fast answers to if your L&D efforts are going to make a big impact on your organisation and the only way you're going to achieve this is by measuring the effectiveness and impact that your learning initiatives have on the business.

We always recommend that you use a proven and tested methodology.

There are a few out there but let's look at some of the most common approaches – *we will expand on each of these in* Chapter 5.

The Kirkpatrick Model

This is probably the most famous and common approach for measuring the effectiveness of learning and development.

The Kirkpatrick Model has four levels of evaluation:

- Level 1 – Reaction.
- Level 2 – Learning.
- Level 3 – Behaviour.
- Level 4 – Results.

Reaction

If you use happy sheets or feedback forms at the end of an event, then you're most likely measuring your learner's reaction to it.

You're evaluating how well they responded to the learning.

For example, questions could include:

- Was the content relevant?
- Was the facilitator engaging?
- Was it pitched at the right level?
- Was it delivered at the right pace?
- What was the most valuable takeaway?
- How was the training room?
- How would you rate the quality of the elearning?

All these questions focus on an initial reaction to the learning.

Learning

Level 2 is focused on whether learning took place and how much was learnt.

Typical activities could include an assessment, test, or quiz. Some level 2 evaluations include a task of some kind to demonstrate and provide evidence of learning.

Other popular methods include self-assessment, line manager and peer feedback. Interviews, role-play, and observations are also common.

Behaviour

Have the learners applied their new knowledge and skills? This is the question that aims to be answered at level 3.

Are they using the learning and making changes at work?

To evidence this, here are some examples of what could be used:

- 360 and 180-degree feedback.
- Self-reflection and peer-assessments.
- Observations.
- Skills and competency interviews.

One of the most widely used activities for this level is a feedback assessment where staff, peer, line managers, suppliers, customers, and the like, can provide input and comments into what has changed because of the training.

Results

This level is where the rubber meets the road! It's all about whether the learning resulted in the business outcomes and benefits that it set out to achieve.

You'll need access to data pre- and post-learning and be able to link any changes to the training.

For example, if there was an uptick in sales in the weeks immediately after a sales development programme, what evidence do you have to link it to specific techniques and knowledge that was covered in the training? How do you know that it wasn't down to market conditions or something else?

Whenever you use hard data, you need a way to link it back to the learning.

You'll need to ask for specifics from the learners.

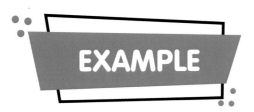

Other Learning Evaluation Models

There are a couple of other models that you can use to help you measure learning transfer.

Phillips ROI Model

One of the most popular is the Phillips ROI model. This model is made up of the four levels of the Kirkpatrick Model and then Phillips is added to it to make up a 5th level.

The Kirkpatrick/Phillips model looks something like this:

The Phillips model uses an equation to calculate the return on investment of learning and development activities.

ROI % = (£ Benefit of Training - £ Cost of Training) / Cost of Training

The equation is the benefit of the training, minus the cost of the training, divided by the cost of the training, multiplied by one hundred. That gives you the return on investment as a percentage increase or decrease.

Here's a quick illustration of this equation:

Imagine that you have just engaged a training provider to deliver a leadership development programme to 40 managers and the total cost of the programme was £45,000.

Your department then interviewed all the managers and gathered hard data from all the resources available to work out what all the benefits were.

Here are some of the benefits that occurred over a 6-month period:

- 5% time saving in a particular task = £35,000 (40 managers x £17,500 salary for 6 months x 5%).
- 3 contracts renegotiated with a saving of £20,000 due to techniques covered on the programme.
- Normal number of leavers across 40 teams would be 25 staff. Actual number of leavers was 9. (Saved 16 recruitment agency fees of £4,000 per head) = saving of £64,000.

Based only on those 3 benefits above we can pop them into the equation.

164% ROI = (Benefit £35k+£20k+£64k – Cost £45k) / Cost £45k

The Kaufman Model

This model is a little like Phillips in that it adds a fifth level to the Kirkpatrick model. The Kaufman model is all about evaluating and measuring the impact and effectiveness of training on different groups. *Full model on page 72*

The CIRO Model

CIRO stands for context, input, reaction, and output. The way it differs to say, Kirkpatrick, is that it focuses on measuring criteria before AND after a learning and development initiative or resource. *Full model on page 77*

The Brinkerhoff Model

This model focuses on comparing the successes of a learning event to its "failures", it looks at successful case studies and examples from the training and compares them to the least effective. All this feeds into recommendations of what to do and what not to do in the future to sustain success. It's referred to as the Success Case Method. *Full model on page 83*

The Anderson Model

Known as the Value of Learning model, it focuses more on the effectiveness and evaluation of an organisation's learning strategy rather than the evaluation of learner effectiveness. It's more about aligning an organisation's learning strategy with their overall business strategy. *Full model on page 88*

Learning Transfer Evaluation Model (LTEM)

The LTEM model was inspired by a piece of learning research. More of the emphasis with this model is geared around the transfer of learning. *Full model on page 93*

What contributes to successful Learning Transfer?

There are two main things:

1. The **support and resources** available to help implement learning pre and post learning event.

2. The **relevancy** of L&D courses and resources to roles and outcomes

Let's take a closer look at each one.

Support and Resources for Learning Transfer Activities

Here are some activities which will help with the transfer of learning:

- Peer to peer coaching.
- Line manager observation.
- Internal mentoring.
- Ongoing assessments and quizzes.
- Regular refreshers.
- Company frees up time for practice.
- Ongoing support groups.

- Online chat groups.
- Social learning.
- Regular 360 feedback.
- Quarterly surveys of what you have embedded.
- Self-assessment.
- Goal setting and review.
- Ongoing training needs review.
- Positive learning culture (this is up to your organisation).
- Practice and modelling.
- Lifelong learning promotion.
- Career goal alignment.
- Job connection links with learning and outcomes.

Relevancy of Learning

Below I've compiled **fifteen approaches** you might incorporate within your training methodology and resources to make them more relevant.

There are many more you might try, but these are among the most popular:

1. Keep it Real

In all your materials, courses and resources ensure that you include real life examples that directly relate to daily challenges that your learners face in their roles.

One of the most common reasons why learners seem disengaged is that the lessons being taught aren't felt to be relevant or applicable.

Common objections voiced might be "that's all very well, but in the real world...". In interactive sessions, have learners provide their own examples for the topics under discussion.

2. Make it Personal

Include examples from your company. This helps build trust and a rapport between the learner and the course leader or resource.

Personal stories help ground the learning and remove some of the distance between the theory and the practice.

3. Ask Questions

Make sure you pause to assess how much is being absorbed at various stages of the learning process.

Simple questions can be posed to course attendees to garner insight into what's been understood. Assessments and quizzes help with online learning.

4. Answer Questions

Make sure you give permission for learners to ask burning questions during live sessions. It's not enough to permit them to approach you afterwards, since the question may have proven directly pertinent to the topic in hand.

By not sharing this moment with the group an opportunity is missed. Ask for attendees to raise a hand so you can choose an appropriate moment for interruption. Use the chat facility and hand up facility for virtual training sessions.

If you're offering online sessions, then ensure there's a mechanism where learners can ask questions.

5. Allow Time for Reflection

It's important not to rush through a course or learning resources.

Some knowledge will take time to digest within the minds of your learners. Allow time for these moments to sink in and become personalised.

6. Introduce Variation

Aim to provide a blended learning approach to cater for different styles and preferences.

7. Use Mixed Media

Engage all the senses of participants by using text, images, animation, video, sound, objects, games, and other means to help embed the learning.

8. Continuity

If you have an on-going programme of modules to deliver then make sure that at the start of each module, some time is set aside to thoroughly review what has been tried back in the workplace.

Ask for successes and failures and what extra support is required.

9. Make a Game of It

Anything you can do to instil a bit of fun into the learning experience will help.

Even something as simple as a quiz can make learning more enjoyable. Hybrid or eLearning models are especially good for this purpose, since they can leverage all manner of online games and interactivity to gamify the experience.

10. Leverage Competitiveness

Related to the above point, breaking groups up into team exercises, whether explicitly competitive or not, will help motivate individuals to participate more fully, engage better and remember more of the topic at hand.

With an online model, offering the opportunity to retake quizzes, increase performance scores or win badges can be remarkably effective.

11. Learn from Students

Humble educators are popular ones – allow for gaps in your own knowledge and allow attendees to supply their own teachable moments where appropriate.

Get a discussion going and you'll find participants are already engaging in active learning transfer.

12. Practice Transference

There may be opportunities to ask learners to recap previous lessons to one another, which helps you monitor how well learning has been imprinted at the same time as instilling learning through practice.

13. Use Storytelling

Metaphors, fables, and illustrative stories help enrich what could be otherwise dry lessons. Aesop knew this in 560BC when he encoded simple moral lessons in amusing children's stories, such as The Hare and the Tortoise, whose lesson about arrogance and perseverance lives on to this day. If 2500 years of continuous learning transference doesn't prove the power of narrative, then what does?

14. Assign Homework

This may not prove a popular suggestion, but making learners think about and employ some of their new skills whilst they are between sessions can help impress learning.

We know that one of the key components of learning transference is repeated practical application, so the more opportunities learners must test out their skills the better. As ever with such strategies, less is more.

15. Read Feedback Forms

Too often such assessments are obtained in lip service to the notion of improvement. However, if you've made it possible for learners to be open and honest, you'll always get some helpful feedback which will allow for improvement in subsequent sessions and resources.

You may choose to do an evaluation midway through a longer programme, as well as one at the end. Always ensure that such forms are submitted anonymously. It doesn't matter who said what, but it does matter what was said.

Create a Learning Culture to Help Transfer the Learning

All these tips are all well and good but if your organisation hinders rather than helps your efforts then you will be facing a losing battle from the start.

The organisations that promote and value learning and development do far better than those who see it as just an expense.

To do this, it's important that you have a learning culture.

There are measures you can take to help with this, and they will ultimately help to maximize the chances of real learning transfer occurring.

Here are just five suggestions:

1. Create a Culture of Constant Learning

Too often eLearning is just a suite of courses that participants feel obliged to "tick off" so that they can return to their daily work. Instead, if the learning is built around what each employee needs to improve, it will be perceived as more beneficial.

When learning is incorporated as a regular part of employee's roles, it will not be seen as an irritating adjunct.

To do this, from day one, an organisation needs to express a belief in the value of constant study and improvement.

Learning content can include newsletters, webinars and other "refreshers" which focus on practical aspects of employees' roles, as well as organised programmes.

The important thing is that the process of learning is cyclical, and learners see marked improvements when they use the lessons learned. Here's where the measurement of learning metrics will benefit both management and employees alike.

2. Incorporate Learning within Development

The completion of training, and the consequent improvement in performance, should be incorporated within appraisals and career progression. This will help promote attendance, engagement, and adherence.

Provide hybrid or eLearning models which can be engaged with at employees' own speed and dipped into in short bites to ensure that learning fatigue does not set in.

3. Customised Development

Rather than buying-in readymade programmes that only tangentially connect with employees' work, why not devise bespoke learning with practical outcomes?

The flexibility of hybrid programmes is that employers can devise unique combinations of guest speaker webinars, group sessions, online programmes, and exercises which constitute a close fit with regular tasks.

Include a practical project which takes a real piece of work and applies a new skill or approach to it. This helps demonstrate how useful the programme can be.

4. Have Line Managers Follow-Up

Assuming managers are up to speed with course content and resources, they can follow up to ensure that new skills are being used within the workplace. This should be done in a supportive rather than disciplinary mode.

If learning hasn't been applied, then an opportunity to refresh key skills can be provided. The approach should be encouraging, rather than punitive, with rewards and appreciation given to those who do demonstrate dramatic performance improvement.

5. Socialise Your Learning

Online forums or Slack channels can be useful. Learners can share the skills they have developed, ask questions, and offer feedback. This can be particularly helpful where the programme has been presented largely online, since it builds a group dynamic.

Such forums also leverage a bit of competition, with participants wanting to outdo one another in terms of performance improvement.

Learning Transfer should be the goal

As we've covered in this chapter, when learning can be transferred, this means it has been fully internalised and absorbed by each learner, then applied in practice.

There are ways of measuring learning transfer and allowing for your L&D efforts to be better aligned both with corporate strategy and individual employee priorities.

Workplaces need to design their suite of learning and development activities for maximum practical applicability. Ideally, everything that you do should be built with minimal gaps between learning sessions and the direct application of newly gained skills.

By following the approaches outlined above, you give your L&D initiatives the best chance to have a wide-ranging impact which is strategically aligned with corporate goals, and which participants take part in enthusiastically that ultimately leads to better business outcomes and performance.

Chapter 4

How to Create a Learning Culture that Drives Performance

"If you can link learning to performance improvement and organisational goals, everything else falls into place."

Sean McPheat

It's becoming increasingly important for organisations to encourage continuous improvement and learning throughout their entire enterprise.

These days, potential employees seek out progressive places to work, which comes down to the culture of your organisation and a learning culture in particular.

There's a growing and significant trend towards continuous professional development (CPD). In some professions (e.g. the law and medicine industry) it's a must, but CPD and continuous learning is now a popular strategy in many other companies too.

The benefits of CPD are also backed up by data:

- 94% of employees admit they'd remain longer at a company which invests in their professional development. [source: LinkedIn]
- 86% of employees say it's important for employers to prioritise their learning opportunities. [source: Ceridian]
- Almost half (46%) of survey respondents say they are bored at work due to a lack of learning and development opportunities. [Source: Udemy]

The statistics above are without even considering how having employees learning new skills can benefit the bottom line.

What then, is the secret to creating a work environment and a workforce that are focused on continually learning and growing?

This lies in the development of a continuous learning culture.

What is the definition of a learning culture?

Put simply, this is an environment in which continuous learning and improvement is provided, welcomed, and eagerly participated in.

Companies who merely pay lip service to mandatory, one-size-fits-all training produce employees who grow to resent training, because they can't see its relevance and it **doesn't have a significant impact on their performance.**

It doesn't meet their training needs.

However, where training and development does benefit employees, by helping them gain valuable skills or perform their roles with greater ease, it is generally welcomed.

A culture of learning is predicated upon four things:

1. Relevant development that is linked to performance improvement.
2. Motivated employees who understand what's in it for them to improve.
3. Supporting managers who are on-board all throughout the organisation.
4. A culture of "coaching" rather than "telling".

If any of the above are missing, then you'll struggle to build a learning culture!

In a continuous learning culture, training and educational programs are built-in to work schedules, rather than being shoehorned into an already busy calendar.

Employees who are consuming learning do not leave their colleagues in the lurch with unbearable workloads.

Instead, the whole environment is built around regular upskilling.

Definition of a Learning Culture

Research firm CEB (part of the Gartner group) gives this apt definition for Learning Culture (as reported in HBR):

"A culture that supports an open mindset, an independent quest for knowledge, and shared learning directed toward the mission and goals of the organisation."

The important components of a continuous learning culture, therefore, include:

- Open mindset - employees are willing to learn new skills and abilities.

- Independent quest for knowledge - employees' learning is self-motivated and does not require constant supervision.

- Shared learning - nevertheless, employees can share what they learn.

- Fit to organisational goals and mission - learning is relevant and profitable.

If you can **link learning to performance improvement and organisational goals,** then most of everything else falls into place.

All too often organisations try to focus on motivational techniques and gimmicks when really, they are missing out on one fundamental concept – performance.

21 Tips for creating a Learning Culture

I've mentioned the importance of linking learning to performance improvement and that it's **THE MOST IMPORTANT** element of creating a learning culture.

Organisations attempt to build a learning culture yet miss out that fundamental mission critical task.

Assuming that you're not one of those, here are 21 ways to help embed that learning culture throughout your organisation.

1. Promote Knowledge Sharing

Use your LMS and create opportunities for people to share their individual skills and knowledge.

Whether it's by hosting weekly skill-sharing sessions or using an online learning platform to post helpful documents and summaries, there are a range of ways to promote the sharing of information.

2. Audit your Skill Gaps

Rather than using educated guesswork, survey the current state of knowledge, skills, and behaviours within your workforce, so that you can readily identify skill gaps.

You'll then be able to better target resources, time, and systems towards filling those gaps.

Creating an organisational needs analysis is a prerequisite for creating training needs and ultimately linking learning to performance requirements.

3. Go Modular

A lot of the frustration employees experience with training programs is how irrelevant many of them seem.

Historically, training took place in groups where programs had to be designed to cover a wide pool of existing skills and knowledge. Now, however, with learning moving online, it ought to be possible to render programs far more specific and focused.

Why run through the history of computer programming and software development, when what you really need to know is how to go about building an app? Creating topic-specific modules rather than broad-based programs will also help keep training aligned with corporate priorities.

4. Align Learning with Leadership

Leadership training can be tied to achieving learning thresholds in a way that benefits executives and departments alike.

Tying advancement to learning is a great way of motivating continuous professional development – it's a carrot rather than a stick.

5. Engage Managers and Supervisors

Rather than making managers feel disadvantaged by having employees removed from the workplace to engage in learning, find ways to involve managers directly in the commissioning of training and development opportunities.

Motivate managers to create spaces for knowledge sharing or positively incentivise their employees to attend.

Of course, listening to what managers say their staff need is key to bringing them on board.

6. Reward IMPACT

You attend a training course, and you receive a certificate. Just for turning up or taking the course!

I see posts on LinkedIn about how Joe Smith is proud to have taken a 1-day course in management. So what? It doesn't tell you how well they did or what impact they made!

Instead, create certificates for impact and for the benefits that the training has made back in the workplace.

Take this one step further and use online badges and public recognition.

7. Position your LMS.

Position or re-position the purpose of your LMS. Move away from usage to performance.

8. Keep it Short and Simple

There's little as off-putting in a piece of coursework as thick reams of text and paragraphs that seem to never end.

Break up your insights with illustrations, photographs, and diagrams.

Further divide your content into mini modules that can be completed in a matter of minutes. This allows even those who are highly time-constrained to make meaningful progress. Being able to pause and come back to a topic later takes some of the pressure off.

9. Encourage Innovation and Experimentation

An environment where risk-takers are rewarded, and new ideas are welcome is usually more conducive to meaningful learning than one in which change is avoided.

Encourage everyone to keep up to date with new systems and radical developments. Learning about new developments can be a lot of fun and can keep your organisation ahead of the curve.

10. Enlist and Create Subject Matter Experts

Alongside using off-the-shelf content and general programs, you should also make sure that some of your training is devised and run by subject matter experts.

These could be in-house personnel if the skillsets are there.

It's much easier to learn from someone who clearly knows what they are talking about and loves the subject matter.

Creating a team of internal subject matter experts will help with creating learning champions throughout your organisation.

11. Learning is a Two-Way Process

Make sure your learning activities have a degree of interaction.

Voicing an idea, thought or understanding will always help to make it "stick".

12. Gamify the Lessons

As well as the rewards and public incentives mentioned above, using quizzes at the end of modules, or at the midway point can help instil key takeaways while gamifying the process of learning. Make sure these quizzes are not too difficult and that participants can go back and revise things they have forgotten, then try again.

After all – it's not actually about the quiz, but about making sure that key points are remembered. Learning that fades away as you read isn't learning at all.

13. Get Hands On

Any activities which can incorporate an activity or project really should.

Engaging the creativity, imagination and practical skills of participants is a great way of making the learning experience memorable.

14. Ensure Accessibility

To avoid leaving anyone out, make sure your learning is accessible to those with mobility issues or sensory impairments.

The last thing you want to do is exclude anyone at your organisation and prevent their learning and development.

15. Give Participants Feedback

Another way to create a culture of learning is to give participants regular feedback on how they are doing.

Even though this may not be delivered publicly, even an encouraging message or email can work wonders with engagement.

When an employee needs to work a little harder or spend more time on a specific area of learning, it's better to be honest and address this sooner rather than later without singling them out.

Putting off giving feedback can lead to colleagues racing ahead and your team ending up at different stages of your learning program. Subconsciously, what the presence of honest feedback says is "this process matters to us; it should to you, as well."

16. Build a Resources Library

Appreciate that not everyone learns the same way. While some like to read, others like to work from instructional videos, podcasts, or in-person seminars.

Start building an accessible resource library where every employee can supplement their understanding of the topic in a manner they enjoy and most benefit from.

17. Consider creating Self-Development Groups

Particularly on the topics of innovation, process improvement, and leadership, there are a great many inspirational resources and books that apply to the business environment either explicitly or implicitly.

Consider setting up informal groups and assigning a piece of learning for discussion.

18. Make it Social.

Affiliated to the self-development group idea is any social learning event where participants are encouraged to mix and interact either online or offline.

Lunch and learn sessions presenting short topics for discussion followed by may work very well for some industries. Consider it a pan-corporate networking session. At many company-wide training sessions employees may meet one another for the first time or continue building on existing working relationships.

19. Make it Ongoing for Everyone

Rather than seeing learning as something which has a concrete duration and an endpoint, begin to promote it as an ongoing process.

Ensure that managers and executives engage as fully as each other.

Education, particularly on a cutting-edge topic, can prove a great leveller.

20. Measure and Adapt

Good training is never static – it evolves to suit both the environment and its participants' needs.

As much as possible, use metrics and KPIs to measure its effectiveness and the degree to which the learning points "stick" and that the transfer of learning back into the workplace has taken place.

Methods such as the Kirkpatrick Evaluation Method can prove invaluable.

Once you've measured the success of your training, you can adapt and change learning methods and content accordingly.

21. Keep it Fun!

Here's an often overlooked but important point to finish with.

Learning doesn't need to be dry or mundane. It can be participatory, and even revelatory. Consider visits to parts of the company too few people see. If you're working for a broadcaster, for instance, take your staff to climb a transmission tower (while learning about relevant broadcast technology, of course). There's an equivalent immersive experience in every industry if you're sufficiently creative.

Chapter 5

Learning and Development Evaluation Models

"Kirkpatrick is not the only game in town".

Sean McPheat

How do you go about measuring the effectiveness of your learning and development solutions?

And what do you measure?

Do you use a proven methodology or are you measuring just the quality and reaction to the training?

And at what level do you measure?

For example, Kirkpatrick measures a learning event. The Anderson Model measures if your learning strategy and organisational goals are aligned.

Many L&D departments that I come across use feedback forms and surveys to evaluate how well the training was received, the quality of the learning, if it was pitched at the right level and delivered at the right pace.

All too few, survey how the learning was transferred and the impacts and tangible benefits that have resulted in the workplace.

You may have heard of the Kirkpatrick training evaluation model before because it's widely used but there are several other models out there – there's more options for evaluation than just the Kirkpatrick model.

Let's look at some of the common and not so common models that could help you measure the impact of your learning solutions.

The Kirkpatrick Model

The Kirkpatrick Model is a widely used, four-level training evaluation method that benefits both learners and L&D teams by allowing them to understand the value and impact certain training has had.

Donald Kirkpatrick first published his ideas about training evaluation in 1959, but it wasn't until 1975 when he further defined them in his book, Evaluating Training Programmes, that they began to command industry attention.

Since then, awareness of his ideas has gradually increased and has been bolstered by a redefinition and update in his 1998 book, Evaluating Training Programs: The Four Levels.

The rest as they say is history, and today, Kirkpatrick's Evaluation Model has arguably become the industry standard within the learning and development community.

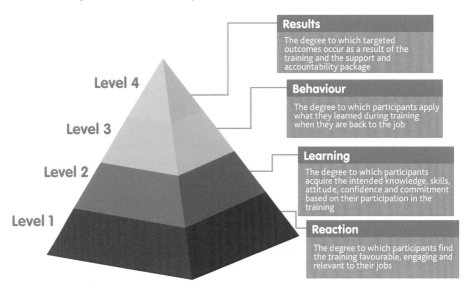

Level 4

Results
The degree to which targeted outcomes occur as a result of the training and the support and accountability package

Level 3

Behaviour
The degree to which participants apply what they learned during training when they are back to the job

Level 2

Learning
The degree to which participants acquire the intended knowledge, skills, attitude, confidence and commitment based on their participation in the training

Level 1

Reaction
The degree to which participants find the training favourable, engaging and relevant to their jobs

What are the Four Kirkpatrick Levels of Evaluation?

1. Reaction

The extent to which learners find the training agreeable, relevant, and engaging.

Learner satisfaction levels are usually assessed using a feedback form or survey, often referred to as a 'Happy Sheet'.

Verbal reactions and post-training surveys can also be used to assess reactions.

What's great about this level of assessment is that it's quick, easy to do and inexpensive.

2. Learning

The increase in knowledge and capability experienced by the learner.

This is usually assessed by conducting and comparing the results of tests carried out before and after training.

Assessment can also be done via interview or observation.

Like Level 1, it's relatively easy to set up and is useful for assessing quantifiable skills.

3. Behaviour

The extent to which learners apply their learning in the working environment.

Compared to Levels 1 and 2, Level 3 requires much more participation and skilled observation from line managers.

Behaviour is assessed via observation and interview over a period to assess behaviour change, how relevant that change is, and whether it is sustained.

You can also measure improvements in behaviour via 180- or 360-degree feedback.

4. Results

The overall impact that the learner's performance has on the business or working environment. This represents a fundamentally different challenge to levels 1 to 3 as individual assessments are carried out.

It's about relating the learner's behaviour change to real bottom-line improvements and organisational performance metrics in a credible and believable way.

A unit of change in learning should be directly linked to a specific improvement in a key organisational metric.

Kirkpatrick Model Examples

It appears a sound and attractive theory, so how does a willing L&D practitioner apply the Kirkpatrick Model in the workplace?

Let's take a look.

Kirkpatrick Level 1 Evaluation Examples

Even though Level 1 Evaluation, (training feedback forms), are unlikely to raise an eyebrow in the boardroom, they should not be dismissed as lightweight.

They have an important role to play in helping you develop engaging training, without which learning will be impaired, and the higher levels of training evaluation will be compromised.

For example, a lack of post-training learning from Level 2, might be due to poor training delivery that can be easily identified in Level 1.

Key criteria that you'll be looking to assess in Level 1 can include some of the following examples:

- Did the venue meet your expectations?
- Did you receive the pre-programme joining instructions?
- Were the joining instructions helpful?
- Were the learning activities engaging and practical?
- What are your 3 key takeaways from the event?
- What is the first thing you're going to work on?
- How will you embed the learning during the role?
- Did you feel the event was a good use of your time?
- Overall, would you say the training was a success?
- Did the trainer cater for your learning style?
- Was the content relevant to your role?
- What the content delivered at the right pace?
- Was the programme delivered at the right level?
- Was the programme too hard or too easy?
- Was the programme covered in the right amount of detail?
- Did the trainer use a variety of different methods?
- Rate the trainer's overall presentation skills.
- Rate the knowledge level of the trainer on the topics.
- Was the trainer flexible to your needs?
- How helpful was the trainer?
- Would you recommend the course to others?

Once you have collected all the data, it's crucial that you act on it where appropriate, delivering constructive changes based on feedback and suggestions from your learners.

Kirkpatrick Level 2 Evaluation Examples

Level 2 learning evaluation looks at knowledge acquisition.

You can also make modifications to Level 2 evaluation processes, by incorporating modern gamification tactics and processes.

By gamifying this part of the evaluation process using leaderboards and badges; you can reward learning and create a healthy sense of competition that will boost learner engagement and learning too.

Interestingly, the way that you assess and recognise knowledge acquisition in Level 2 can ultimately enhance learning.

The following are examples of what can be used to measure the learner's knowledge:

- Self-assessment
- Peer assessment
- Quizzes
- Role-play
- Interview
- Observation

Kirkpatrick Level 3 Evaluation Examples

This level of learning evaluation comes with significantly greater challenges than Levels 1 and 2.

You'll need to look at how well your learners have modified their behaviour because of the training they receive.

Are they applying the learning in practice?

You'll also need to be aware that behaviour change can only be expected to happen in a conducive environment.

For example, let's say that you miss out Level 1 and 2 assessment and just focus on post-training office behaviour and note that no behaviour modification has occurred.

It would be easy to assume that the training didn't work and that the learners didn't learn anything.

This could indeed be the case, but it could be that learning did take place, but the learners are simply not applying it.

There are various reasons why learning might not be applied, such as the manager not allowing them to apply the new knowledge, or not providing supporting opportunities for them to practice.

The reasons can also be more intrinsic such as the employee having no desire to apply the knowledge or lacking the confidence.

An important ongoing enabler of Level 3 evaluation is, therefore, to create a work environment that promotes the application of new learning.

Managers should be actively encouraged to consider linking reward and recognition programmes to applied learning by awarding and publicly praising staff for deploying new skills, techniques, and behaviours.

Managers will have a big role to play in creating a learning culture in their organisation that involves longitudinal observation and data collection.

Despite this, managers are also under time pressures and may need learning professionals for support to devote time to motivating line-managers to prioritise this activity.

In Level 3 you'll be looking to answer some key questions:

1. Have the learners applied any of their learning?
2. Are learners able to train others with their new knowledge, behaviour, or skills?

3. Do learners seem aware that their behaviour has changed?

For Level 3 evaluation to be successful you'll need to get managers on-board and make the evaluation process as effortless, easy, and straight-forward as possible to carry out.

The following are examples of what can be used to measure the learner's behaviour change:

- Self-assessment.
- Peer assessment.
- 360-degree assessment.
- 180-degree assessment.
- Role-play.
- Skills interview.
- Competency-based interview.
- Observation.
- Evaluators.

Kirkpatrick Level 4 Evaluation Examples

In practice, the final stage of the Kirkpatrick Model of Evaluation will require the biggest investment of time and resources.

You need to make a credible link between macro benefits, otherwise known as results in the business, and specific training, to assess the true organisational impact of that training.

The kind of outcomes you may consider trying to link training to are:

- Increased productivity.
- Lower staff turnover.
- Increased customer satisfaction.

- Increase staff engagement levels.
- Increased sales revenues.
- Fewer mistakes or less waste.
- Increased compliance.
- Fewer sick days and absence.
- Reduced customer complaints.
- Customer retention rates.
- Recruitment fees.
- Staff satisfaction.
- Reduction in accidents.
- Increased staff morale.
- Increased quality.

CASE STUDY EXAMPLE

Measuring the effectiveness of an online course

A group of managers at a company is taking an online emotional intelligence course on their LMS.

The company wants to evaluate the effectiveness of the course to make sure it's meeting the managers' needs and achieving the intended learning outcomes.

Level 1 - Reaction

The company evaluates the managers' reactions to the course by conducting a post-course survey which is automatically sent via the LMS.

The survey includes questions about the managers' satisfaction, motivation, and interest in the course.

The results show that most of the managers were satisfied with the course, motivated to learn about emotional intelligence, and found the course interesting.

Here are some of the high level "scores on the doors" from the survey:

Was the course:

Helpful to you	85%
Relevant to your needs	90%
Delivered at the right pace	91%
Pitched at the right level	88%
Interactive	84%

Level 2 - Learning

The company evaluates the managers' acquisition of knowledge and skills by administering pre- and post-course assessments.

The assessments include multiple-choice and true/false questions that measure the managers' recall and comprehension of the emotional intelligence concepts.

The results show that the managers have improved their knowledge and understanding of emotional intelligence.

Area	Pre-Score	Post-Score	Improvement
Self-awareness	73%	96%	23%
Self-regulation	66%	90%	24%
Social skill	85%	98%	13%
Empathy	70%	96%	26%
Motivation	82%	92%	10%

Level 3 - Behaviour

The company evaluates the managers' application of the knowledge and skills they have learned by observing their behaviour during team meetings, and by measuring their ability to manage conflicts and improve team cohesion.

The observations and measurements show that the managers are applying the emotional intelligence concepts effectively and that the team cohesion and performance have improved.

A 360-degree feedback activity was also conducted comparing the managers behaviours before the course and then 3 months after it. 30 statements were measured, 6 for each of the EQ areas. Results below:

Area	Pre-Score	Post-Score	Improvement
Self-awareness	65%	96%	29%
Self-regulation	67%	97%	30%
Social skill	70%	89%	19%
Empathy	58%	88%	30%
Motivation	85%	94%	9%

Level 4 – Results

The company evaluates the overall impact of the online emotional intelligence course on the organisation by measuring the employee satisfaction and retention, and the overall productivity and quality of the teams.

The results show that the employee satisfaction and retention have increased, and the overall productivity and quality of the teams have improved.

Improvements in % terms:

Time savings	12%
Self-confidence	23%
Employee satisfaction	18%
Staff retention	10%
Error rates	31%

Limitations of the Kirkpatrick Evaluation Model

Let's look at some of the potential limitations of using the model for training evaluation.

Level One: Reaction

Self-assessment forms are necessarily subjective, and learners may be completing them in haste so they can get back to their desks, leave work for the day or just because they don't have time. In addition, any focus group exercises conducted by the training provider may suffer from the learners' natural bias towards pleasing the trainer.

On the other hand, if learners are given post-study surveys much later, when its more convenient and possible for them to be objective, there is the risk that the training won't be as fresh in their mind.

Another type of bias that needs to be combatted is the tendency for learners to rate their experiences based on how they concluded, rather than averaging out their experiences over the whole duration of the training.

Level Two: Learning

When assessments are performed following training, they further eat into the time that learners must make themselves available. It can be expensive to run assessments, and not all learners will perform as well in standardised tests, since anxiety levels, memory, reading ability and cognitive skill all play a part in how well one can perform during an assessment.

Another way to run such assessments is during the training, with a short quiz after each component or module. Most online training requires participants to complete brief tests on each topic before moving on to the next, to avoid participants having to complete lengthy tests at the end.

Level Three: Behaviour

Here's where evaluation can become extremely time-consuming and challenging, since it requires ongoing, periodic observation. A manager may simply not have capacity to engage in this sort of oversight.

Even where they do have time, and the necessary enthusiasm to devote themselves to the task, such behavioural studies generate reports which usually require actions to be taken.

There's also the question of how to avoid skewing the results, should staff become aware they are being assessed. Finally, it requires a level of expertise which a manager might simply not possess. To ensure workplace observations like this are carried out to a high standard, it can be wise to retain the services of the training provider.

Level Four: Result

As with any experiment, you must move from correlation to causation. Just because an improvement has been noted in a particular work area, doesn't mean that training was the precise cause.

Other potential causes might need to be eliminated first, so that you can prove a tangible connection between training and outcome. This requires expertise and a scientific approach to analysis. Doing this level of evaluation could again prove time consuming and costly.

If it occurs too far in time from the training, there's a danger its relevancy will be questioned. It's also possible that corporate strategy may have moved on to other concerns.

General Limitations

Although it has been updated, the Kirkpatrick Model is now more than sixty years old. It was designed for a traditional, active, group training model, whereas a large proportion of training in the 21st century happens individually, during ordinary work activities and virtually.

Despite the caveats presented above, the Kirkpatrick Model for training and development evaluation remains one of the best we have, and it's still widely adopted to validate training endeavours.

The Phillips Model

The Phillips ROI Model is often considered to be the fifth level of the Kirkpatrick Model.

The Kirkpatrick Model focuses on evaluating the reaction, learning, behaviour, and results of a training or development program. The Phillips ROI Model focuses on evaluating the return on investment (ROI) of the program.

The ROI calculation is a financial measure that assesses the economic value of the program, by comparing the costs of the program to the benefits that it generates.

The ROI calculation is a way to demonstrate the impact of the training or development program in financial terms, and it's the way to show the organization if the program is worth the investment.

By adding the Phillips ROI Model as a level 5 to the Kirkpatrick Model, organisations can not only evaluate the effectiveness of the program in terms of reaction, learning, behaviour and results, but also assess the economic value it has generated for the organisation, by comparing the costs of the program with the benefits generated, this allows the organisation to make more informed decisions about the future of the program, whether to continue, modify or discontinue the program.

The Level 5 evaluation equation looks a little like the following:

ROI % = (£ Benefit of Training – £ Cost of Training) / Cost of Training

CASE STUDY EXAMPLE

How does Level 5 work in practice?

Here's a case study example to help you get a feel for this model.

Let's say that by introducing a new eLearning system packed full of sales training and resources you have increased sales by 10% which yielded an additional £100,000 in profit.

This £100,000 is our £ Benefit of Training.

Then, you need to identify how much your training cost. Let's say that your LMS implementation costs and yearly subscriptions are £20,000.

Also, you needed to train 50 salespeople on the system with an hourly charge out rate of £100 an hour for an hour's training, at a total lost opportunity cost of £5,000.

This means your £ Cost of Training is £25,000.

If we run all these figures through the Phillips equation, you're left with your ROI figure to impress the boardroom.

In this case, it's a 300% ROI, recouping three times the original investment in training.

ROI 300 % = (£ 100,000 – £ 25,000) / £25,000

This is quite a simplified look at the ROI calculation and there are greater levels of detail and refinement that will need to be explored in real-world practice.

As you would imagine, this analysis would ordinarily be deployed retrospectively as confirmation of the effectiveness of your training intervention for purposes of recognition and securing future budgets.

However, the equation also plays a role in planning as it can be used to develop ROI forecasts and projections and enable your organisation to make more informed training investment decisions.

The Kaufman Model

Roger Kaufman first introduced his model of evaluation "Kaufman's Five Levels of Evaluation in the publication of 'Levels of evaluation: Beyond Kirkpatrick' in 1984.

The model is positioned as being *"more practical"* than Kirkpatrick's and aims to be a *"more effective approach to evaluation"*.

At its core it's regarded as being an extension and development of the Kirkpatrick Model of Evaluation as it is very similar in its evaluation processes. One key difference, however, is that Kaufman's model splits Kirkpatrick's first level 'Reaction', into two:

* **Input.**
* **Process.**

And additionally, he also introduces a fifth level **Societal Outcomes.**

His decision to replicate and expand on Kirkpatrick's original 'Four Levels' is a strategic decision to help gain acceptance from those familiar with Kirkpatrick by not rocking the boat too much.

Let's dive in and look at the steps in more detail.

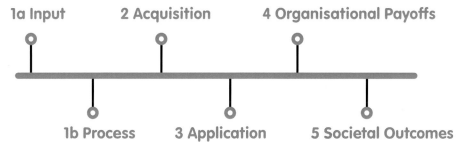

1a Input   2 Acquisition   4 Organisational Payoffs

1b Process   3 Application   5 Societal Outcomes

The 'Five' Levels of Kaufman's Learning Evaluation Model

1a. Input

The first step focuses on the measurement of resources. To assess what resources are available and used to support the training and the coaching.

In a world full of quick and easy access to digital resources, this step highlights the importance of evaluating the quality of the resources that are being used. Quite simply, what is the quality of the training resources - *could they be better, what else is out there to take inspiration from?*

Workshops and research are key during this step to ensure a thorough evaluation of the training resources used.

1b. Process

The second split of the first step, is the evaluation of the overall delivery process.

It encourages evaluation of the efficiency of the training and the acceptability of it amongst learners - what is the learner's experience during the delivery process? What are their thoughts, are they engaged, or are they bored to death?

Survey's, feedback forms or live observation are some key examples of how to go about assessing this stage.

2. Acquisition

This step, referred to by Kaufman as a micro-level, measures how much of the learning is absorbed by the learners.

Some things that come to mind assessing this step, is to hold tests for learners to ensure they have "acquired" and remembered what was in the training.

3. Application

This stage is also referred to as another 'micro-level'.

In this stage the learners would be observed applying what they learnt to their roles around the workplace - *outside of tests.*

This can be monitored through live observation around the workplace - an example being, how does a learner deliver customer service after customer service training.

4. Organisational Payoffs

We then move onto the pay offs for the organisation (the macro-level client) as a whole.

Rather than just evaluate the learner, Kaufman's model also suggests evaluating the impact the training has had on the organisation as well.

For example, has the training generated an improvement in performance across the board, or has it helped with growth/income across the organisation.

Going back to that customer service example, the improvement in customer service has meant more happy customers and higher sales!

I've mentioned before about the importance of performance improvement from learning and this stage measures exactly that. Well done, Kaufman!

5. Societal Outcomes

Kaufman's final step outlines the benefits the training might have on other organisations or society in general.

Does the training transcend out to external business clients and into society? Happier customers, growth in a particular market etc.

Whilst Kaufman's Five Levels of Evaluation may not be everyone's go-to for training evaluation (with Kirkpatrick's taking precedent), the model does offer some additional concepts that can be applied to ensure a thorough evaluation of L&D initiatives.

I like the additional level of societal outcomes because that's all about "becoming more" and having a wider impact on more than just their own organisation.

Let's look at Kaufman's model being used in real life.

CASE STUDY EXAMPLE

Using the Kaufman Model to evaluate a Customer Service Course

1a. Input: At this level, the evaluation focuses on the resources and materials used in the training programme. For example, an evaluation of a customer service course would look at the curriculum, trainers, and facilities used. This level of evaluation would assess whether the training materials were relevant, current, and sufficient.

1b. Process: The focus of this level is on the delivery of the training. For example, you'd look at how well the trainers delivered the content, whether the exercises were effective and whether the learners were engaged during the training.

2. Acquisition: This level of evaluation assesses whether the learners have acquired the knowledge and skills taught during the training. For example, you'd look at whether the learners can correctly answer questions related to customer service best practices and whether they have improved their communication skills.

3. Application: This level of evaluation assesses whether the learners can apply what they have learned in the training to their job. You'd look at whether the learners are able to solve customer complaints more effectively or whether they are providing better customer service because of the training.

4. Organisational Payoffs: This level of evaluation assesses the impact of the training on the organisation like have customer complaints decreased or whether customer satisfaction has increased because of the training.

5. Societal Outcomes: This level of evaluation assesses the impact of the training on society so it would look at whether the training has led to increased customer satisfaction and better customer service, which could in turn lead to increased customer loyalty and economic growth for the company and the community.

It's worth mentioning that level 5 is less common to find it in evaluations as it's more of an outcome and less of an evaluation, but it's still a good measure to consider understanding the bigger impact of the training on the society.

The CIRO Model

One of the lesser-known learning evaluation models out there is the CIRO Model.

Developed by Peter Warr, Michael Bird, and Neil Rackham in 'Evaluation of management training' (1980), CRIO offers an alternative to Kirkpatrick and Kaufman's evaluation models.

That's because it specifically evaluates *management training.* This sets it apart from other models making it a bespoke and niche model. It can be used for other roles, but it's mostly associated with evaluating management and leadership training.

But it does mean it becomes limited in its flexibility as it cannot be used to measure alternative roles and positions around an organisation like a supervisor or sales advisor.

CIRO stands for Context, Input, Reaction and Outcome and like most learning evaluation models it follows a hierarchical structure. This means you would start with Context, then move to Input, and through the others one at a time.

CIRO Model

Context Evaluation	Training need analysis based upon organisation conditions
Input Evaluation	Information about alternative training resources
Reaction Evaluation	Information about the Trainee's reaction to Programme content, Approach and Value added to improve training process
Outcome	Information about the results of Training

It's key to note that in this model, the first three levels are evaluation steps and the last one provides the results.

You cannot see the results without first evaluating the first three steps.

What are the Four Levels of the CIRO Model?

1. Context (Evaluation)

The first step in CIRO is for managers to assess the operational situation that an organisation finds itself in, i.e., what information is there within the organisation to determine the need to conduct specific training. What is the context for the training?

The aim here is to find out what training needs are there, based on the organisation's conditions. For example: sales figures are low, so sales training is needed amongst teams to increase sales.

At this stage a 'training needs analysis' is crucial to determine and outline the objectives to provide substance.

These objectives can be split into three:

Immediate Objective	Intermediate Objective	Ultimate Objective
What can be achieved immediately from the initial training - i.e., the learning of a new skill or knowledge (sales skills training).	What repercussions will come from the training - how can it be harnessed long term. (Change in employee behaviour/ confidence).	How the training can help to eliminate any flaws within the organisation. (a pickup in sales figures /growth).

2. Input (Evaluation)

In the second stage of CIRO, the organisation would need to analyse what 'input' is given during the training.

In other words, how is the training delivered?

This level stresses the evaluation of the training's design, the methods and techniques used to deliver it, and how it is managed.

The aim of this step is to evaluate what resources are being used and inputted into the training whilst exploring other means and training resources that could be adapted to make it even better.

To enable the training to be aligned further with the desired objectives (that were explored and found within the first Context stage).

3. Reaction (Evaluation)

The next stage of CIRO is for the company to engage with learners who have received the training and to ask for their feedback.

The learners are asked to provide their reactions/feedback on the following topics:

1. The content of the training.
2. The approach of the trainer.
3. The value that the training provided.

The information gained during this stage is used to evaluate the success (or failure) of the training directly from the source.

4. Outcome

Finally, now that all the evidence has been collected,

- the context behind the training - *why is the training needed?*
- the input that is needed for the training - *how is the training delivered?*
- the reaction from trainees about the training - *what do learners think of the training?*

It would be time for the managers and the organisation to evaluate the whole package.

To assess the results of the training and whether it was (or wasn't successful). CIRO proposes to do this you need to split the outcome into three categories:

Immediate Level	Intermediate Level	Ultimate Level
How did the learners get on - did they learn something new (skill or knowledge)?	What is going to take a little longer from the back of the training - new design/new method in delivering the training?	Has the training impacted the organisation? Remember the sales training example from earlier.

Let's see CIRO in action.

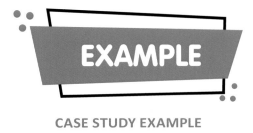

CASE STUDY EXAMPLE

Let's assume an evaluation was carried out. Here is a very brief write up on the findings for 10 managers who have attended a management training course.

Context

The management training course was aimed at improving the managers' skills in delegation, communication, problem-solving, and decision-making. The course was offered to a group of 10 managers. The course was offered because the company had recently undergone a restructuring, and the managers need to improve their skills to manage the changes effectively.

Input

The training programme was designed by a team of experienced management trainers, and the course material included a manual, videos, and case studies. The course was delivered over a period of two days, in a training facility that was well-equipped with the necessary technology and resources.

Reaction

The managers participated in pre-training and post-training surveys to provide feedback on the course.

The survey results indicate that the managers found the course to be well-organised and relevant to their needs, and that the trainers were knowledgeable and engaging.

Outcome

The company conducted a follow-up survey to assess the impact of the training on the managers' performance.

The survey results indicate that the managers have improved their skills in delegation, communication, problem-solving, and decision-making.

Additionally, the managers' report that they can manage their teams more effectively, and the teams are performing better as a result.

The company also noted a decrease in errors by 13% and an increase in productivity, 22%, which can be correlated to the training.

The Brinkerhoff Model

The Brinkerhoff Model is one of the more recent methods of evaluating training.

Also known as the Success Case Method (SCM), the framework was introduced in 2003 by Robert Brinkerhoff.

At its core the model aims to find out how a training or coaching programme works well (or why it's not working) by focusing on the best and worst learners who have participated in the training. The model does not concern itself with 'average performance of learners' like other models or all learners in general. *A little niche but it still sees results.*

Alongside this, SCM provides an entirely different way of evaluating training by placing a strong focus on qualitative analysis. Instead of surveys, or assessment data, SCM encourages the creation of stories off the back of discussions with specific learners.

Quality over quantity, right?

The main goal of SCM is to identify and interview the most and least successful participants of the learning and then compare the differences between them.

To find this out the following five steps are proposed.

01
Identify a course, resource or programme and it's intended outcomes or impact for evaluation

02
Create an impact model that defines what success looks like

03
Identify the most and least success cases

04
Conduct interviews with the most and least success cases and document why they performed well or not

05
Document and share the output, stories and impacts. Identify successes, lessons and create a way forward

The 5 Steps of The Brinkerhoff Model

1. Plan

Determine what programme or course you want to evaluate.

2. Define

Make an impact model for the programme/course and define what success should look like for learners taking part in the programme/course.

3. Identify

Create a survey/feedback form or any other method to identify the most and least successful learners.

For example, who scored the most/least on a test initiated directly after the training.

Or who enjoyed the training most/least? Who thought they got the most out of it?

4. Document

Conduct interviews off the back of the findings with the most and least successful learners and document why they succeeded/failed or why they enjoyed/didn't enjoy the training. Bring in supporting evidence.

5. Conclude and Recommendations

Communicate your findings with any relevant parties involved - HR, L&D teams - and share the lessons learnt. From here you can make any recommendations for improvement or hold group sessions to improve the training.

By focusing on the best and worst learners, Brinkerhoff's SCM implies that 'success' can easily be identified.

The worst learners can provide evidence of flaws in the training that led them to fail - *things that might have been missed or things that need more clarification for example.*

Whilst the best learners can provide evidence of what is going well for them to have succeeded - methods/*tools used that helped them succeed or any specific resources that cemented the information.*

By drawing on the extremes of best and worst, Brinkerhoff suggests that the model can help to identify what is really happening in the training, and how the training can be improved.

One of the key strengths of the Brinkerhoff Model is that it provides a clear and systematic approach for evaluating development projects and allows improvements to be identified early on, which can help to increase the chances of success.

Additionally, the model is flexible and can be adapted to different types of projects and contexts, making it suitable for a wide range of development initiatives.

CASE STUDY EXAMPLE

Here's an example of how the Brinkerhoff Model could be used to evaluate an emotional intelligence course.

Plan

The emotional intelligence course was aimed at improving the learners' emotional intelligence skills, with a focus on self-awareness, self-regulation, motivation, empathy, and social skills.

The course was being offered to a group of 10 managers from a variety of departments within an organisation.

The course was being offered because in a recent survey the results illustrated that the managers of the organisation need better communication skills, more self-awareness and that they don't demonstrate any empathy to their people.

Define

The success of the programme was going to be based on the quality of the design and the delivery of the programme and specific results were to include improvements in employee retention and staff satisfaction.

In addition, post training 360-degree feedback would highlight if the manager's emotional intelligence areas were improving.

Identify

The defining stage involved assessing the current emotional intelligence skills of the managers.

This was done through assessments, which revealed that most of the managers had a basic understanding of emotional intelligence but needed to improve their ability to apply the concepts in their work environment.

Additionally, the best and worst learners were identified, where best learners were those who had high emotional intelligence and worst learners were those who had low emotional intelligence.

Document

The documenting stage involved interviewing the best and worst learners who providing feedback on the content, materials, and activities for the course.

The course was delivered over a period of two days and was well-received by the two learners. They found the course to be well-organised and relevant to their needs, and they felt they learned a lot from the training even though they were at both ends of the spectrum.

A follow-up survey was conducted to assess the impact of the training on the learner's emotional intelligence. The survey results indicate that the worst learners have improved their emotional intelligence, particularly in the areas of self-awareness, self-regulation, motivation, empathy, and social skills. Additionally, the company also reports an increase in employee satisfaction of 11% and employee retention of 17%, which can be correlated to the training.

Conclude

The programme was deemed a success with real tangible results and was also designed and delivered in way that resonated to the learners.

It was recommended that this programme was rolled out to all managers within the company and also an employee version of the programme so everyone within the 120 workforce could benefit from higher levels of emotional intelligence.

The Anderson Model

First published by the Chartered Institute of Personnel and Development in 2006, The Anderson Model is relatively new to the training evaluation industry.

Unlike some of the models explored up to this point, The Anderson Model is designed for evaluating learning at organisation level, the bigger picture, rather than specific learner levels participating in the training.

Sometimes referred to as Anderson's Value of Learning Model, it aims to align an organisation's learning solutions with its strategic priorities.

The model was originally inspired by a study into learning and development benchmarking by Brandon Hall. The study found that organisations expectations for learning and development were not closely aligned to their business goals.

In other words, organisations were failing to ensure the right development programmes were being initiated to ensure business growth and success long term.

Anderson's model focuses on addressing issues like this over 3 stages and helping to evaluate what is important to an organisation and what is the right training that needs to be implemented at the right time.

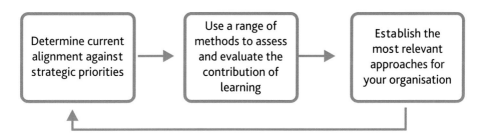

What are the stages of The Anderson Model?

Stage 1: Determine current training against strategic organisation goals

To start with, the model aims to determine the current alignment of the learning that you offer against the strategic priorities for your organisation. To review what training is currently being conducted and whether it's aligned with the overall goals of the business.

So, for example, your strategic priorities for your organisation might include:

- Aggressive sales growth of 25%.
- Increased production of 15% (to be aligned with the point above. Supply and demand).
- To reach a new market within Europe.
- Reduce staff of attrition of 18% down to less than 10%.

The question is then this:

"To what extent are your learning and development solutions supporting these priorities and are they focused on them?"

Is everything aligned and joined up?

If there's not a sales development programme in place or some kind of sales academy where your salespeople continually upskill and improve then how will your organisation reach, it's aggressive sales growth target of 25%?

Stage 2: Assess and evaluate the contribution of The Learning

Within this stage it evaluates the contribution and role that learning, and development has on your organisation.

The model is not prescriptive when it comes to this, but it does identify hour key areas that should be evaluated and measured:

- **Learning and Development function measurements**
  - o How effective is your L&D function?
  - o How effective and efficient are your L&D team members?
  - o How effective are the trainers and any sub-contractors or external suppliers that you use?

- **Return on expectation measurements**
  - o Do your learning and development solutions deliver what they were intended to deliver? i.e. improved sales by 10%, better team morale?
  - o Have the expectations of your solutions been met? Did they achieve what they set out to achieve?

- **ROI measurements**
  - o Cost v Benefit analysis. i.e., sales training costs £120,000 but the uplift in sales was £1.2 million.

- **Benchmarking measurements**
  - o How does your learning and development solutions, processes and their performance outcomes compare to previous periods both internally and externally?
  - o How does your solutions compare to external factors, competitors, and standards?

Stage 3: Establish the most relevant approaches

The final stage is to develop a plan of action that suits your organisation.

There are many factors to consider when determining this and how your organisation positions learning and development.

For example, I've come across thousands of organisations who believe wholeheartedly that they are doing the right thing by offering learning solutions whereas thousands of others view learning as a cost to the business.

Go figure!

The emphasis and importance that you place on metrics and the type of metrics will determine what approaches you use. It's a unique and personal thing to your organisation.

For example, some organisations want a quick return. Others, play the long game.

And it's whether your organisation is focused on the short- or long-term benefits of learning and development and whether your stakeholders and organisation as a whole values learning, ultimately determines what metrics you will want use.

This can be summarised in the table below:

	Senior management trust in the learning contribution ⌄	The organisation requires learning value metrics ⌄
Emphasis on the short-term benefits ❯	Learning Function Measures	Return on Investment Measures
Emphasis on the long-term benefits ❯	Return on Expectation Measures	Benchmark & Capability Measures

I really like Anderson's Model because it's focused on the organisation and not on a specific learning event like Kirkpatrick and Phillips for example.

Anderson is all about measuring and developing a learning and development strategy that is linked to organisational performance improvement – just like what this book is all about.

There's room for both!

On a micro level you could use Kirkpatrick and at a macro level you can use Anderson.

The Learning-Transfer Evaluation Model (LTEM)

First introduced by Dr. Will Thalheimer in 2018, The LTEM states that "training has only been successful when the learner applies the learned material in their behaviour" and he identified 8 tiers for evaluation.

LTEM: Learning-Transfer Evaluation Model

Tier 8	Effects of Transfer	Work
Tier 7	Transfer	Work
Tier 6	Task Competence	Learning
Tier 5	Decision-Making Competence	Learning
Tier 4	Knowledge	Learning
Tier 3	Learner Perceptions	Learning
Tier 2	Activity	Learning
Tier 1	Attendance	Learning

What are the 8 Tiers of LTEM?

Tier 1 - Attendance

The first/bottom tier is where the learner signs up/attends a learning experience or training of some sort.

Whilst important to look at and assess, ultimately, there's no emphasis on the results because a learner might attend a course but not necessarily learn anything from it.

Tier 2 - Activity

The learner engages in the training experience and takes part.

Important considerations:

- Attention - Are learners paying attention?
- Participation - How much are learners getting involved - interacting with trainers/the group/the session?
- Interest - Are learners interested in the material?

Equally, observing the learner's activity during the activity is part of the process, but a learner could pay attention, get involved and show interest. That does not mean they have learnt anything.

Tier 3 - Learner Perceptions

At Tier 3 you would question the learners about the training they had taken part in to gain insight into how effective it was for them.

You could do this through feedback forms, surveys etc.

In today's world this is where most organisations stop according to Thalheimer.

However, the results at tie 3 only determine the effectiveness of the training and whether the learner is going to take away and use the knowledge/skills gained.

Tier 4 - Knowledge

A measurement of how much of the training the learner has remembered.

To do this a test is either initiated either during or at a later date where the learner answers questions about facts/terminology of what was delivered during the training.

Tier 5 - Decision Making Competence

The learner makes decisions given relevant realistic scenarios - i.e., roleplay or any other form of testing where what was taught can be put into action.

This is not just the testing of facts/terminology of the training, but the doing of what was taught.

Tier 6 - Task Competence

The learner is tested and performs relevant realistic actions and decision making to determine how competent they are with the new skills they have required.

For example, utilising the facts/terminology that have been taught and the doing and putting the skills into action successfully.

Tier 7 - Transfer

The seventh tier is to measure when a learner uses what was learned to perform work tasks successfully on a day-to-day basis.

Thalheimer places a stronger importance on this part of the process compared to the other previous tiers.

That's because this tier determines whether the participant can apply the learned material to accomplish tasks successfully (also known as 'transfer').

Are they able to transfer the learning into everyday work?

Tier 8 - Effects of Transfer

The last tier measures the effects of 'Transfer'.

What are the effects of the transfer on the (a) learners, (b) co-worker, family, and friends, (c) organisation, (d) community, (e) society, and (f) the environment.

What impact has the training had beyond the learner?

Whilst this is like Kaufman's 5th step 'Societal Outcomes', Thalheimer is more thorough in assessing the journey from the learning/activity, all the way through to the societal outcomes.

Thalheimers LTEM essentially is based on the idea that the goal of training is to be able to improve performance on the job. To not just absorb information but to be able to actively transfer the skills into work and beyond.

Chapter 6

Aligning Learning to Performance: 50 Questions to Ask Yourself

"It's time for you to make your own impact!"

Sean McPheat

The purpose of this final chapter is to get you to start thinking about how you could implement some of the concepts and ideas from this book.

Yes, the purpose of this book was to improve your performance as well!

I'm going to your virtual coach in this chapter and ask you lots of questions.

These questions will act as thought starters and set you on your way for making the shift from focusing on usage and consumption and moving to a performance focused ethos in terms of your learning and development strategy and solutions.

Now, I'm not going to provide space for you to write your answers because there will be a lot of blank pages, but instead I'm going to list them down under headings.

Ready?

Have fun. Oh, and by the way, you should be able to provide hard evidence for each question not just hearsay.

Aligning Learning to Performance

How is your learning and development strategy currently designed? What is the process?

Is your learning and development strategy aligned to your overall business objectives and goals?

Is your learning and development strategy evaluated against the business objectives? i.e., it achieved what it set out to achieve.

Are your learning and development activities effectively addressing the skills and knowledge gaps of employees? (How do you know this?)

Are your learning and development activities resulting in measurable improvements in job performance and business results?

Are employees engaged and motivated to participate in learning and development activities within your organisation?

Are your learning and development activities being delivered in a timely and cost-effective manner?

Is there a clear process for evaluating the effectiveness of your learning and development activities?

Are your learning and development activities being continuously reviewed and updated to stay current with the evolving needs of your organisation?

Are there any changes or improvements that can be made to your learning and development strategy to better align it with the business objectives?

How is the progress tracked against the goals and objectives of your learning and development strategy?

How has your learning and development strategy contributed to the overall performance of the company?

Do you have specific goals and objectives for each of your learning and development solutions?

Which of your learning and development solutions are most effective?

Could you summarise on one sheet all the impacts that learning and development has made on the business? All rolled up into headings like reduced costs, increased sales, reduced attrition etc.

Do you have a learning and development mission in place that is linked to your organisation's mission and values?

Are your learning and development solutions centred around solving real business problems?

Do your employees understand where your learning and development function adds value?

Does your organisation have a learning culture?

Are employees encouraged to continuously learn and develop new skills?

Is learning and development a priority for your organisation, and is it reflected in the budget and resources allocated for it?

Are managers and leaders actively involved in promoting and supporting a culture of learning within the organisation?

Are employees provided with opportunities for continuous learning and development, such as training programmes, LMS, workshops, and e-learning courses?

Is there a clear process for identifying and addressing skill gaps within the organisation?

Are employees given the freedom and flexibility to pursue their own learning and development interests?

Is there a culture of sharing knowledge and best practices within the organisation?

Are employees rewarded and recognised for their efforts in learning and development?

Is there a system in place for gathering employee feedback on the effectiveness of learning and development programmes?

How is learning and development tied to performance evaluations and career development?

How is learning and development tied to the performance of teams, departments, and business units?

Repositioning your LMS

How is your learning management system currently perceived?

- By you
- By L&D
- By line managers
- By learners
- By key stakeholders

What do you focus on the most with your LMS when it comes to evaluation and measurements?

What is the objective of your LMS?

What role does your LMS play in the overall strategy of your organisation?

How does your LMS capture impacts and tangible results?

What resources does your LMS provide to help transfer the learning back to the workplace?

What is the ROI for your LMS?

Do learners understand the impact that your LMS is making?

Learning Evaluation Models

Which of the learning models covered in this book have you heard of before?

Which models have you tried?

Which of the models are best fit for your organisation and why?

Which of the models could you trial for an upcoming learning event or a resource that are low risk so you can evaluate its impact and effectiveness?

Do you mostly focus on reaction level evaluation?

Do your key stakeholders place importance on evaluation and measurements?

Does your organisation think short term or long term when it comes to the benefits from learning interventions?

Do you mostly focus on learning event evaluation rather than learning and development as a whole?

The Last Word

So that's a wrap!

I hope I have given you some food for thought. It's now time for you to make your own impact and that starts with measuring the impacts that your learning and development function are making.

Armed with this, you can demonstrate and prove all the good you're doing to help develop your people and ultimately improve organisational performance. This will ringfence L&D as a mission critical department and will revolutionise how you're perceived within the business as performance improvement experts.

Sean McPheat – CEO

If you're looking for a **learning platform and/or content,** we can help. Skillshub is a **modern-day learning platform** that grows with you.

No matter where you're starting from, Skillshub will be able to support you and your learners to help them improve their performance.

Not only is our platform one of the **easiest to use,** you'll also be able to **create personal learning journeys** at the drop of a hat, matching the needs of your people to the **thousands of learning and digital assets** that are loaded onto the platform.

If you're looking for **engaging content** for your current learning management system, we can help you with that as well.

We can **support you** in any of the following ways:

Please **contact us today** for a **FREE demo** or to **discuss your requirements** in more detail with one of our team.

Contact
Web: **www.skillshub.com**
Email: **info@skillshub.com**
Phone: **02476 998 101**